SCHOLASTIC SCIENCE READERS™

LEVEL
3
AGES 7 AND 8

W9-BFQ-114

WOLVES

by Carolyn B. Otto

SCHOLASTIC REFERENCE

PHOTO CREDITS: Cover: Erwin & Peggy Bauer. Page 1: Carl R. Sams II & Jean F. Stoick/ DPA (Dembinsky Photo Associates, Owosso, MI); 3: Charlie Ott/Photo Researchers; 4 & 5: Richard Hamilton Smith/DPA; 6: Claudia Adams/DPA; 7: A. & J. Visaoe/Peter Arnold, Inc.; 8: Carl R. Sams II & Jean F. Stoick/DPA; 9: Bud Lehnhausen/Photo Researchers; 10: Claudia Adams/DPA; 11: Erwin & Peggy Bauer; 12: Stan Osolinski/DPA; 13: Erwin & Peggy Bauer; 14-15: Dominique Braud/DPA; 16: Carl R. Sams II/DPA; 17: Erwin & Peggy Bauer; 18: Dominique Braud/DPA; 19: Skip Moody/DPA; 21: S. J. Krasemann/Peter Arnold, Inc.; 22: Charlie Ott/Photo Researchers; 23: Tom & Pat Leeson/Photo Researchers; 24: Bruce Montagne/DPA; 25: Erwin & Peggy Bauer; 26: Dominique Braud/DPA; 27 & 28: Tom & Pat Leeson/Photo Researchers; 29: Erwin & Peggy Bauer; 30: Mark J. Thomas/DPA; 31: Christie's Images; 32-33: Michael P. Gadomski/Photo Researchers; 34: Lance Beeny, North Logan, UT; 35: W. Perry Conway/Corbis; 36: Lynn Rogers/Peter Arnold, Inc.; 38: Ryan Hagerty/United States Fish & Wildlife Service, AP/Wide World Photos; 40-41: Willard Clay/DPA; 43: George Gentry/USFWS; 44 & 45: Jim Roetzel/DPA.

ISBN 0-439-16295-5

Book design by Barbara Balch and Kay Petronio

20 19 18 17 16 15 14 13 12   05 06 07 08

Printed in the U.S.A. 23

First printing, September 2000

We are grateful to Francie Alexander, reading specialist, and to Adele M. Brodkin, Ph.D., developmental psychologist, for their contributions to the development of this series.

Our thanks also to our science consultant Chuck Miller, zookeeper at the Cheyenne Mountain Zoological Park, Colorado, and to Tom Zieber for the introduction to his wolf friends at Mission: Wolf near Westcliffe, Colorado.

In the North, a gray wolf trots
across the Alaskan tundra.

His slender legs carry him easily. Wolves are travelers, made for long distances. The top speed of a running wolf approaches 30 miles (48 kilometers) an hour.

At a trot, a wolf may cover 20 or 30 miles (up to 48 kilometers) in a day. But journeys of more than 100 miles (161 kilometers) in twenty-four hours have been reported.

The gray wolf, though, is not going so far, not today. He will stay near the **den**, the summer home of his **pack**. During this time of year, there are **pups** to be watched over, pups to be cared for and fed.

Wolves are social animals. A wolf pack is mostly made up of family. Though a pack might be just a pair of wolves, it can also number a few dozen.

An average wolf weighs somewhere between 80 and 100 pounds (35 to 45 kilograms). A wolf may measure up to 3 feet (1 meter) tall at the shoulder.

Take a Closer Look

Close-up of a wolf's paw print

At first glance, a wolf looks a lot like a husky dog or a malamute.

Most scientists agree that our dogs are descended from wolves.

A long time ago, at least 12,000 years, humans began to **domesticate** (duh-**mess**-tuh-kate) wolves. People raised wolf pups and they kept the tamest ones.

Very slowly, over thousands of years, the babies of pups raised by humans changed and grew much tamer. Though wolves will always be wild animals, domesticated wolves gradually became the dogs we know today.

gray wolf

When he comes to a creek, the gray wolf wades in to drink.

The paw prints
he leaves in the
mud seem huge.
The wolf shakes the
water from his fur,
and then goes on.

The Alaskan tundra is beautiful.
There are hills and rocks and grasses,
and small flowering things, but no
tall trees.

Just under the ground's surface,
the soil is frozen. Even in summer,
the air is chilly.

It is very cold here for humans in the winter, but a wolf can turn around and around to make a bed in the snow.

He will protect his nose with his bushy tail, and go to sleep in temperatures of 30° to 40°F (34° to 40°C) below zero.

Wolves come in many colors—white, gray, black, tawny, golden-red.

In the cold months, the wolves
blend in with the winter landscape.
When they hunt, they are like ghosts
in a world of white.

The wolf stops to sniff at a bush to one side of the path. It has served as a **scent post** for some time.

He lifts a leg and leaves his mark. The smell tells the pack he has been here, and it will warn strange wolves away. Scientists call this **scent marking**.

In the last hour, the wolf has eaten a number of mice, voles, and lemmings. He chased, but didn't catch, a swift-footed arctic hare. On his way back to the den, the wolf's ears prick forward. He pounces on a mouse.

The inside of a wolf's den

The pups are happy to see him. They whimper and lick at the big wolf's mouth. In response, he throws up, or regurgitates (ree-**gur**-juh-tates), some partly digested meat. In the wild, animals often must bring food home in their bellies.

The wolf's mate is the color of
coffee. Her eyes are very bright. They
touch noses. She is five years old; the
male is six.

Three more young wolves form the pack, all pups from seasons before. Whining, tails wagging, they greet their father.

Wolves howl in a way that is almost like singing. They yip, yap, whimper, whine, and bark. Wolves talk or communicate in other ways, too, with scent marking and with the way they move their bodies.

A wolf might wiggle and wag in an invitation to play. Or he may roll over on his back to show he means no harm. This kind of communication is often called body language.

Each wolf has a special place in the pack. The leader is usually a male, and the other wolves in the pack will follow him as they hunt, as they eat, and in play. It is the leader's mate who chooses the site for the den, and the other wolves will stay nearby.

For the first two or three years of their lives, young wolves remain with their pack. Then they may go off to find mates and start families of their own.

Once there were wolves all across North America. You are probably living in a place where wolves once roamed.

Back then, there were great herds of caribou (**kar**-i-boo) in the Northlands. To the south were moose and elk and deer, and bison on the plains.

Native American wolf mask

Wolves hunted these animals, and so did Native Americans. Though they sometimes hunted wolves and used wolf fur for clothing, many of their stories show wolves as equals, as powerful spirits, as friends, and as teachers.

When the European colonists came to North America, they brought different ideas about land and about wolves. They built houses and barns. They built pens to keep their farm animals, or livestock, in. They killed wolves to keep their animals safe.

Over time, the new settlers slowly
tamed the land. As cows and horses
and sheep replaced bison and deer, as
fences began to mark the places where
one person owned this and another
that, the wilderness was changed
forever. It became at last the towns
and farms and cities we know today.

When wolves could no longer hunt native animals, they turned to hunting livestock. Then people hunted wolves. They caught wolves in steel traps. Wolves were shot or they were poisoned (**poi**-zuhnd). Other animals ate the poison and died, too—foxes, coyotes, badgers, bears, eagles, ravens, and more.

Take a Closer Look

Close-up of a wolf trap

Wolves were killed to protect livestock. And wolves were also killed for their fur, which was made into warm clothing. Wolf hunters collected bounties—they were paid for each wolf they killed.

All across America, wolves were dying out. They disappeared from the East and almost completely from the South. The plains wolves and western packs vanished. In many parts of the country, wolves were seriously endangered.

By the mid-1900s, wolves lived only in Alaska, and in the northern woods of Michigan, Wisconsin, and Minnesota.

Just when it seemed wolves might be killed off altogether, people's ideas began to change. Scientists studied wolves, and they learned more about keeping the **balance** of the hunters to the hunted, of **predators** to **prey**.

Wolves are predators. Predators are hunters and must eat meat to survive. Meat-eaters are also called **carnivores** (**kar**-nuh-vorz). The animals they hunt are known as prey.

Predators are part of the **natural balance.** But the wolves in America were almost gone.

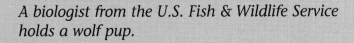

A biologist from the U.S. Fish & Wildlife Service holds a wolf pup.

Yellowstone National Park

So laws were passed in the United States to help native wildlife. One of the most important was the Endangered (en-**dane**-jurd) Species (**spee**-sheez) Act of 1973. This law made it a crime to trap or kill certain animals, including the wolves in the lower forty-eight states.

The laws also tried to protect the places where animals live, like the Alaskan tundra, and to maintain the balance of life in areas of wilderness. It took many years, but wolves were finally brought back to a few places like Yellowstone National Park, on the border where Idaho, Montana, and Wyoming meet.

Wolves have lived free in Yellowstone since 1995. For the most part, they have done what wildlife experts expected. The wolves have hunted deer and elk and bison, and killed the weakest animals. The stronger, healthier animals lived on.

It may be too early to tell, but perhaps the balance is being restored there.

The parents of this wolf pup were brought to Yellowstone National Park in 1995.

In the meantime, far away, the gray wolf raises his head to howl. It is time for the pack to hunt.

When winter comes the pups will be almost grown. They will travel with the pack.

They'll learn to track caribou and to hunt, and to curl up to keep warm in the snow. They'll howl with the others. They'll learn to sing.

Glossary

balance or natural balance—when things even out in nature

carnivores (**kar**-nuh-vorz)—animals that eat meat

den—a cave or a shelter; a home for wolves

domesticate (duh-**mess**-tuh-kate)—to tame, or gradually make a wild animal more useful to humans

pack—a group or family of wolves

predators—animals that hunt and eat other animals; carnivores

prey—the kind of animal a predator hunts

pups—young or baby wolves

scent marking—the process of making something smell, usually by urination

scent post—a shrub, rock, or any place that is used for scent marking

Index

A Note to Parents

L earning to read is such an exciting time in a child's life. You may delight in sharing your favorite fairy tales and picture books with your child.

But don't forget the importance of introducing your child to the world of nonfiction. The ability to read and comprehend factual material will be essential to your child in school, and throughout life. The Scholastic Science Readers™ series was created especially with beginning readers in mind. These books, with their clear texts and beautiful photographs, will help you to share the wonders of science with *your* new reader.

Suggested Activity

A lthough wolves are wild animals, opportunities abound for you and your child to see them in person. There are wolves at the Folsom Zoo in Folsom, California. Illinois residents can see wolves in two locations. "Wolf Woods" is the name of the wolf exhibit at the Brookfield Zoo, and the Scovill Zoo in Decatur hosts "Wolf Howls" on Saturday afternoons. The Como Park Zoo, in St. Paul, Minnesota, also has an exhibit called "Wolf Woods," as does the Cheyenne Mountain Zoo in Colorado Springs, Colorado. The Columbus Zoo in Columbus, Ohio, is home to both gray wolves and Mexican wolves. You'll find gray wolves at Portland's Oregon Zoo, too. Your local zoo may have a wolf exhibit—give them a call and check it out!

No wolves near you? You can investigate the gray wolf recovery program online, sponsored by the United States Fish & Wildlife Service, at: **http://www.fws.gov/r3pao/wolf**